STEP INTO YOUR POWER

Also by Mariëlle S. Smith

52 Weeks of Writing Author Journal and Planner, Vol. I: Get out of your own way and become the writer you're meant to be

52 Weeks of Writing Author Journal and Planner, Vol. II: Get out of your own way and become· the writer you're meant to be

52 Weeks of Writing Author Journal and Planner, Vol. III: Get out of your own way and become the writer you're meant to be

365 Days of Gratitude Journal: Commit to the life-changing power of gratitude by creating a sustainable practice

365 Days of Gratitude Journal, Vol. II: Commit to the life-changing power of gratitude by creating a sustainable practice

Fleshing Out the Narrative: A 31-Day Tarot and Journal Challenge for Writers

Get Out of Your Own Way: A 31-Day Tarot Challenge for Writers and Other Creatives

Set Yourself Up for Success: A 31-Day Tarot Challenge for Writers and Other Creatives

Seven Simple Spreads 1: Seven Simple Card Spreads to Unlock Your Creative Flow

Seven Simple Spreads 2: Seven Simple Card Spreads to Direct Your Creative Flow

Seven Simple Spreads 3: Seven Simple Card Spreads to Boost Your Confidence

Seven Simple Spreads 4: Seven Simple Card Spreads to Celebrate Your Creative Wins

Speak Your Truth: A 31-Day Tarot Challenge for Writers and Other Creatives

Tarot for Creatives: 21 Tarot Spreads to (Re)Connect to Your Intuition and Ignite that Creative Spark

Co-written under the pen name Heather Maclee

Too Good to Be True?

Where There's a Will

There's a Way

Step into your power

A 31-day tarot challenge
to unleash your creative potential

Mariëlle S. Smith

ISBN 978 94 93250 05 5

When you step into your power and your true authentic self, you shine. You shine so brightly that the world tries to keep up.

Shannon Kaiser

INTRODUCTION

Welcome to *Step into Your Power*, a 31-day tarot challenge for writers and other creatives ready to unleash their creative potential.

The thirty-one daily prompts in this book will help you to better understand your relationship to power, where and why you haven't stepped into your creative power (yet), and how you can harness or reclaim that power without becoming overpowering yourself.

Step by step, you will unravel:

- how you relate to notions such as 'power' and 'empowerment',
- where and why you've been giving your (creative) power away, and
- what steps you need to take to fully step into your creative power.

At the end of the challenge, you will be ready to take control over your creative expression and unleash the full force behind your creative potential.

Doing a tarot challenge

So, how does a tarot challenge work? Quite simply. Each day, you pick up your deck of choice, shuffle to your heart's content, and pick a card or more, depending on the question and what your gut tells you. The next day, you put the card(s) back into your deck, shuffle like you mean it, and pull out your next draw.

I only suggest the number of cards you could be drawing on occasion, but you should feel absolutely free to draw as many as you like no matter what day or question. Your gut always knows best. Likewise, it doesn't matter how you shuffle your cards or decide which card is the one that needs picking. Just go with what you've been taught or feels right for you in this moment. There's really no doing this wrong.

The same goes with how you interpret the cards' messages. Some feel utterly comfortable using the guidebook that came with their deck, while others rely solely on their intuition. You can do either or a bit of both: when doing a reading, I don't mind glancing at the description offered by the creator of the cards, especially when I feel there is more to a card but I just can't seem to grasp the full meaning of it at the time. The guidebook won't always bridge that gap, but it might just give you another perspective, that 'Aha, of course!' moment that will kickstart your intuition. Whatever you do, don't let others tell you what is right and wrong: there's only a right and wrong for you, and you will know what is what in the moment.

I highly suggest that you write down your findings and reflect on them as you go. The same card might show up again and again: what could that mean? Some cards will
only make sense later, after you answer a few more questions. Reflecting on previous draws will be especially relevant in those cases. And, even if all the cards make perfect sense the moment you draw them, looking at the bigger picture might still reveal something you hadn't considered before. It's in the reflecting that the wisdom lies.

Use whatever works for you

Those familiar with my work know that I don't differentiate between means of divination. I might use the word tarot, but you can use any deck of cards, whether that be tarot, oracle, or angel. If you'd rather use your crystals or your runes, feel free to go with that.

Those familiar with my work know that I don't differentiate between means of divination. I might use the word tarot, but you can use any deck of cards, whether that be tarot, oracle, or angel. If you'd rather use your crystals or your runes, feel free to go with that.

For those who want to do the challenge but aren't comfortable using either of those divinatory tools, or simply don't own any, use each question as a journal prompt. Sit down in a quiet space, take a few deep breaths, and let whatever answers need to bubble to the surface come.

Likewise, if you would like to mix things up—perhaps the one question makes you want to grab your favourite oracle deck, while another makes you pick up a notebook—please do. Your challenge, your rules. As long as you follow that gut of yours.

DAY 1

How do I relate to the concept of power?

DAY 2

How do I relate to the idea of empowerment?

DAY 3

How do I relate to the notion of willpower?

DAY 4

How did I relate to the concept of power as a child (card 1) and how has this influenced how I relate to power now (card 2)?

DAY 5

How did I relate to the idea of empowerment as a child (card 1) and how has this affected how I relate to empowerment now (card 2)?

DAY 6

How did I relate to the notion of willpower as a child (card 1) and how has this impacted on how I relate to willpower now (card 2)?

DAY 7

What is the current state of my willpower?

DAY 8

What has diminished my willpower in the past?

DAY 9

What currently diminishes my willpower?

DAY 10

How can I harness or reclaim my willpower for the present (card 1) and for the future (card 2) without becoming overpowering?

DAY 11

Think of two to three people who have used their power in a way that inspires you. Draw a card for each, asking: 'What are the seen aspects behind their actions?'

DAY 12

Return to the people you picked yesterday. Draw a card for each, asking: 'What are the unseen aspects behind their actions?'

DAY 13

Once more, return to the people you singled out earlier. Draw a card for each, asking: 'What can I learn from this person's actions today?'

DAY 14

How much control did I have over my creative output while growing up?

DAY 15

How much control do I have over my creative output now?

DAY 16

When was the last time I gave my creative power away to someone else?

DAY 17

Why did I give my creative power away at that time (card 1) and to this person (card 2)?

DAY 18

When was the last time I felt truly in control over my creative expression?

DAY 19

What was it that made me feel this empowered at the time?

DAY 20

Your power centre is located right above your navel, at your solar plexus. For the rest of the challenge, I invite you to do the following breathing exercise before you draw your card(s).

Place both your hands on your solar plexus and breathe deeply in and out three, five, or seven times. Once you feel centred, direct your focus to the question and draw your card(s).

What does empowered creative work look like to me?

DAY 21

Place both your hands on your solar plexus and breathe deeply in and out three, five, or seven times. Once you feel centred, direct your focus to the question and draw your card(s).

What risks and obstacles are
involved in creating such work?

DAY 22

Place both your hands on your solar plexus and breathe deeply in and out three, five, or seven times. Once you feel centred, direct your focus to the question and draw your card(s).

What do I need to know about these
risks and obstacles?

DAY 23

Place both your hands on your solar plexus and breathe deeply in and out three, five, or seven times. Once you feel centred, direct your focus to the question and draw your card(s).

When looking at my creative work, where haven't I fully stepped into my own power yet?

DAY 24

Place both your hands on your solar plexus and breathe deeply in and out three, five, or seven times. Once you feel centred, direct your focus to the question and draw your card(s).

If you singled out multiple areas yesterday, draw at least one card for each.

What is keeping me from fully stepping into my own creative power here?

DAY 25

Place both your hands on your solar plexus and breathe deeply in and out three, five, or seven times. Once you feel centred, direct your focus to the question and draw your card(s).

How can I let my own creative work empower me without becoming overpowering myself?

DAY 26

Place both your hands on your solar plexus and breathe deeply in and out three, five, or seven times. Once you feel centred, direct your focus to the question and draw your card(s).

What are the first actual steps I can take to fully step into my own creative power?

DAY 27

Place both your hands on your solar plexus and breathe deeply in and out three, five, or seven times. Once you feel centred, direct your focus to the question and draw your card(s).

What fears do I have around these steps?

DAY 28

Place both your hands on your solar plexus and breathe deeply in and out three, five, or seven times. Once you feel centred, direct your focus to the question and draw your card(s).

What do I need to know about these steps?

DAY 29

Place both your hands on your solar plexus and breathe deeply in and out three, five, or seven times. Once you feel centred, direct your focus to the question and draw your card(s).

Which of these steps can I take today?
Draw a second card for some last-minute advice
and then go take that plunge.

(I'm not kidding, go!)

DAY 30

Place both your hands on your solar plexus and breathe deeply in and out three, five, or seven times. Once you feel centred, direct your focus to the question and draw your card(s).

To reflect on yesterday, draw three cards:

Knowing this about power (card 1), I reclaim my willpower by (card 2), so that I can unleash my creative potential in this way (card 3).

DAY 31

Draw one or two cards and use them to create your own personal power mantra.

Once you're done, I invite you to take a sheet of paper and write your power mantra down. If you'd rather paint or embroider it, go right ahead. Now hang it in a spot where you can see it as you work.

If you feel like sharing, take a picture and send it to marielle@mswordsmith.nl. I'd love to see what you came up with.

PLEASE CONSIDER LEAVING A REVIEW

Authors are nowhere without honest reviews, and I'd truly appreciate it if you left one on Goodreads, my Facebook page facebook.com/mswordsmith, or the retailer where you bought this book.

The Creative Cardslingers

Isn't it better to sling cards together?

Join my private Facebook group The Creative Cardslingers (password **CITRINE**) to meet fellow creative cardreaders, be the first to test my latest card spreads, and hear all about the creative projects I'm involved in.

WANT MORE?

Head over to mswordsmith.nl/starterkit and get my free Get Out of Your Own Way Starter Kit now.

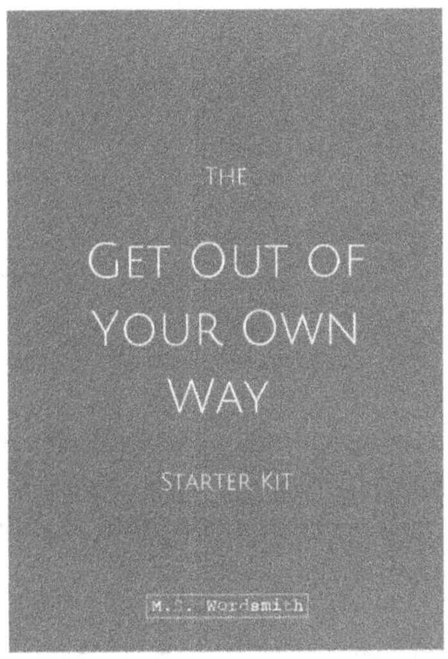

The Get Out of Your Own Way Starter Kit includes four different tools:

- An exercise on limiting beliefs,
- a monthly tracking and reflecting worksheet,
- a meditation on letting go of limiting beliefs,
- a tarot spread on creative roadblocks (from *Tarot for Creatives*),

and is yours when signing up to my newsletter.

ABOUT ME

I'm a coach for writers and other creatives, an editor, a writer, an intuitive healer, and a custom retreat organiser. Born in the Netherlands and raised by my Dutch mother and Scottish expat father, I moved to the island of Cyprus in February 2019.

The thing about being somewhere new is that it sheds a different light on your life. Your mind opens up to other perspectives, and you find yourself brimming with new ideas. Or old ideas you never wanted to take seriously suddenly demand your attention.

Bringing the spiritual into my work was a scary step for me, because I've always tried to keep the two separate. I say 'tried' because quite a few of my clients, and the work they brought with them, have forced me to merge my professional background with my spiritual interests. Some hired me to edit or translate their holistic books, others came to me for coaching and were struggling in a way that needed a broader approach. And then there are the many writers and other creatives who are openly incorporating spirituality into their practice as we speak.

Over the past year, I've switched gears and gradually allowed the spiritual to enter my workspace. This book is one of its many manifestations. It goes without saying that I hope you'll enjoy it, and get from it everything you need.

Want to get in touch? There are different ways and places to contact me:

Website: mswordsmith.nl
E-mail: marielle@mswordsmith.nl
instagram.com/mariellessmith
facebook.com/mswordsmith

ACKNOWLEDGEMENTS

I'd like to thank

ANDRI for not being afraid of my power

my FOLLOWERS for their courage to show up, no
matter what challenge I throw at them